Beyond Sound:
A Deeper Look Into Music

Beyond Sound:
A Deeper Look Into Music

Written By:
Austin Mardon, Ayushma Neku
Laiyba Wasim, HanShu

Edited By: Catherine Mardon

Copyright © 2022 by Austin Mardon
All rights reserved. This book or any portion thereof may not be reproduced or used in any manner whatsoever without the express written permission of the publisher except for the use of brief quotations in a book review or scholarly journal.
First Printing: 2022

Cover Design by Paige Prins
Typeset by Paige Prins

ISBN: 978-1-77369-849-6
eBook ISBN: 978-1-77369-850-2

Golden Meteorite Press
103 11919 82 St NW
Edmonton, AB T5B 2W3
www.goldenmeteoritepress.com

CONTENTS

CHAPTER 1
The Kinematics and Dynamics
of Musical Performance 7

CHAPTER 2
Neuromechanics/Neurology of
Music in Respect to Piano and Violin 19

CHAPTER 3
Music Therapy: Introduction and
Popularization of Music in Clinical
Healthcare Settings.. 31

CHAPTER 4
A Fictionalized Account of the Invention
of the Piano, Interrupted by a Modern
Account of Playing It... 45

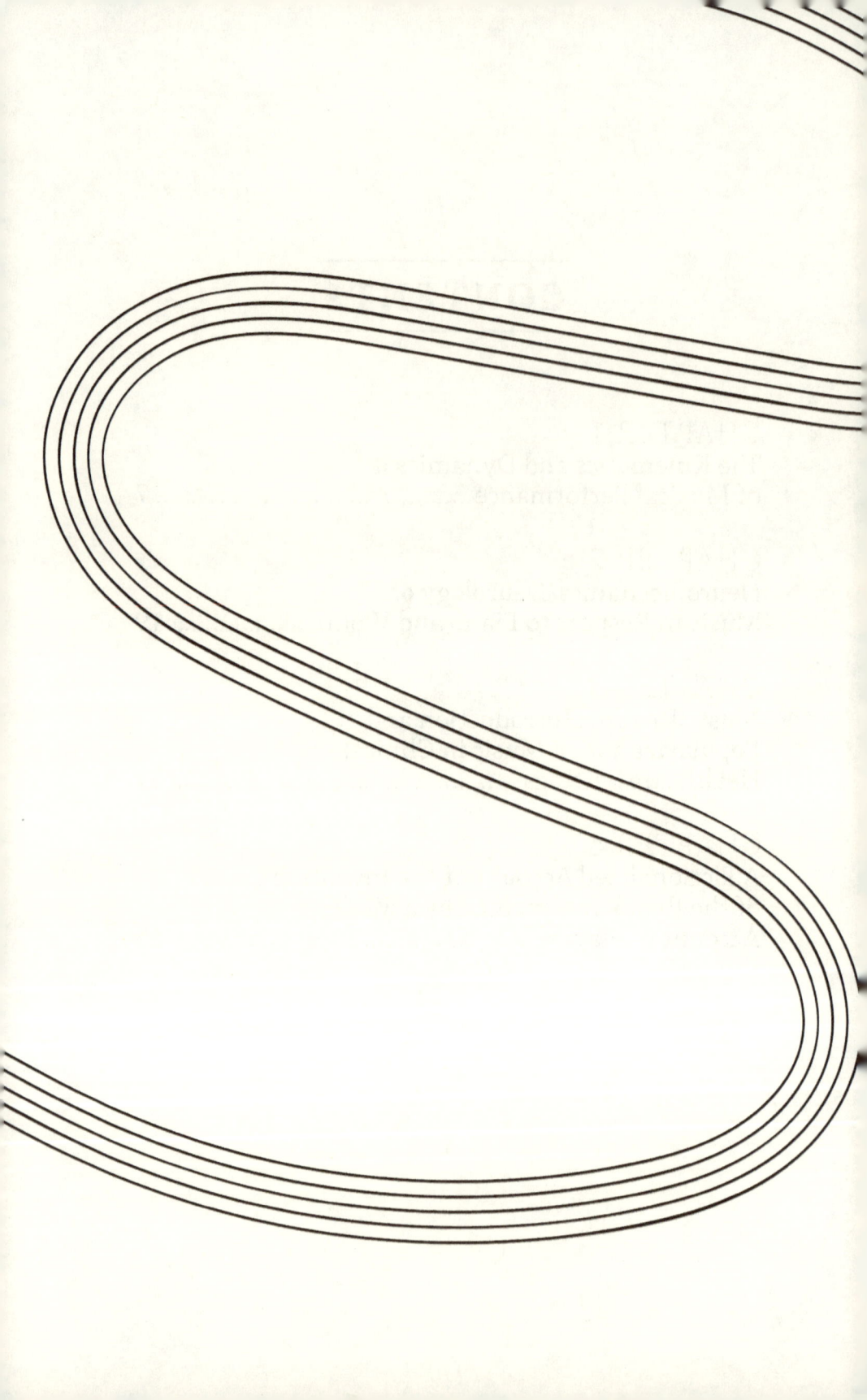

CHAPTER ONE

The Kinematics and Dynamics of Musical Performance

By Ayushma Neku

Introduction

Musical performance is a culmination of sensory, cognitive, and motive coordination including accurate and dexterous movements (Wristen, 2000). The musician adopts changes in anatomical angles, force, speed, and acceleration to achieve a particular musical outcome (Cluss et al., 2006). Understanding these movements provide insight into the neural control of skilled hand and upper limb behaviour (Furuya et al., 2011). Such motor strategies often lead to postural, neuromuscular, and musculoskeletal disorders. Kinematic and dynamic analysis of these motor strategies provides a basis for studying these neurological disorders that exacerbate motor functions.

Degrees of Freedom and Anatomical Complexity

A degree of freedom (DOF) is a concept central to kinematics (Chiaverini et al., 2008). It is defined as the number of directions an object has the ability to move. If an object exists in space, it has six DOF: three translational and three rotational. Mechanical and anatomical systems typically have more than the minimum six. For example, there are 17 joints and 30 muscles in the hand which provide 27 DOF (ElKoura & Singh, n.d.). Increased DOF provides objects such as robots with increased dexterity that minimize joint torques and workspace obstacles (Chiaverini et al., 2008). However, this gives rise to redundancy, where the object possesses more joints than that required to execute its task. No object is inherently redundant; it is the tasks which the object executes that lead to redundant mechanisms.

The human body has anatomically redundant mechanisms (Morasso, 2022). Various combinations of muscular and joint movements can perform the same activity. This kinematic redundancy and neurophysical redundancy provide the basis of the Degree of Freedom problem. The DOF problem poses one main question: how does the nervous system choose task-dependent assemblies of DOF as motor synergies to execute a task? When playing the piano, for example, the biceps aid in lifting the forearm away from the keyboard and shoulder motion (Russell, n.d.). The biceps also play a role in forearm pronation and supination, controlling the palm-down or palm-up position respectively. When the bicep muscle contracts, any of the three motions can occur.

Furthermore, muscles can not push, they can only pull. For any joint to move in two directions, a minimum of two muscles, referred to as an agonist-antagonist pair, are compulsory; one muscle extends and another flexes the joint. Activation of an agonist-antagonist pair can also result in no motion if both exert an equivalent force on the joint.

When learning piano techniques, one aspect is the minimization of limb stiffness. An example of this in piano performance is when a musician supinates their bicep without flexing their elbow. If a third muscle opposes the action of the biceps in flexing the elbow, supination of the forearm will still occur. The activation of the third muscle does not change the resulting movement but increases the net stiffness of the elbow joint. It should also be noted that the biceps crosses the shoulder joint. In order to reduce muscle rotation around the shoulder when the bicep is flexed, the shoulder stiffens. A final layer of complexity is added when considering the role of the brain and spinal cord in choosing which muscle is used for a specific task. The brain selects the muscles that create the desired movement based on past behavioural patterns among other factors.

As can be seen, a simple movement has complex biomechanical implications. Redundancy provides an infinite number of ways that the upper limb can move in order to produce a single-tone. The arms, hands, fingers, and limbs used to play an instrument should not be considered a pure motion or force generator as a result. This is important to keep in mind when analyzing the kinematics of musical performance.

Past Studies: Kinematics in Musical Expression
SIMPLIFIED MATHEMATICS

A set of variables are used to describe the geometry of motion in musical performance (Todd, 1995). The path of a person in movement is modelled by parametric curves, with a spatial coordinate depending on time (an independent parameter). Kinematic equations are a type of parametric equation. When considering limb movements, the variables are represented by either Cartesian position, $x(t)$ and $y(t)$, or joint angles. When considering musical performance, additional variables are considered.

In studies that analyze motion and time, the vertical axis is often described as pitch space (p). The horizontal axis, traditionally representing time, describes the metrical position (x). Using x is inaccurate as a piece of music can have the same "length" but a different speed at which the piece is played (tempo). For this reason, tonal motion and rhythmic motion are defined. Tonal motion accounts for pitch as a function of time p(t) whereas rhythmic motion accounts for the metrical position as a function of time x(t). To simplify, let the motion with one DOF take the metrical position x(t) as the kinematic variable. x(t), v(t), and a(t) represents the position, velocity, and acceleration as a function of time. t(x), v(x), and a(x) are characterized by position; this is useful because various formulations use the metrical position as the independent variable. These variables are related by a system of equations

(Equation 1).

a=a(t), a=a(x)

v=v(t)=a(t)dt, v=v(x)

x=x(t)=v(t)dt, t=t(x)=1v(x)dx

Equation 1: A system of equations that relate x(t), v(t), and a(t). a(x) and v(x) are determined by solving t=t(x) and substituting in v(t) or a(t). This system of equations is derived from the graphs of motion taught in introductory physics courses; they are foundational in kinematics.

Measurement Techniques Used

There are few studies that have recorded the kinematic measurements of musicians (Furuya & Altenmüller, 2013). Existing data is mainly on piano biomechanics, framed by the devices developed to measure such parameters (e.x. Hand movement during piano performance). Measurement techniques (Figure 1) are split into two categories: passive systems that use paint or reflective markers and active systems that use devices requiring a power supply via battery or cable (MacRitchie, 2015). Motion capture via depth camera tracking, paint markers, and infrared are the most common example of a passive system. Examples of active devices include LED position sensors, accelerometers, data gloves, and electrogoniometers.

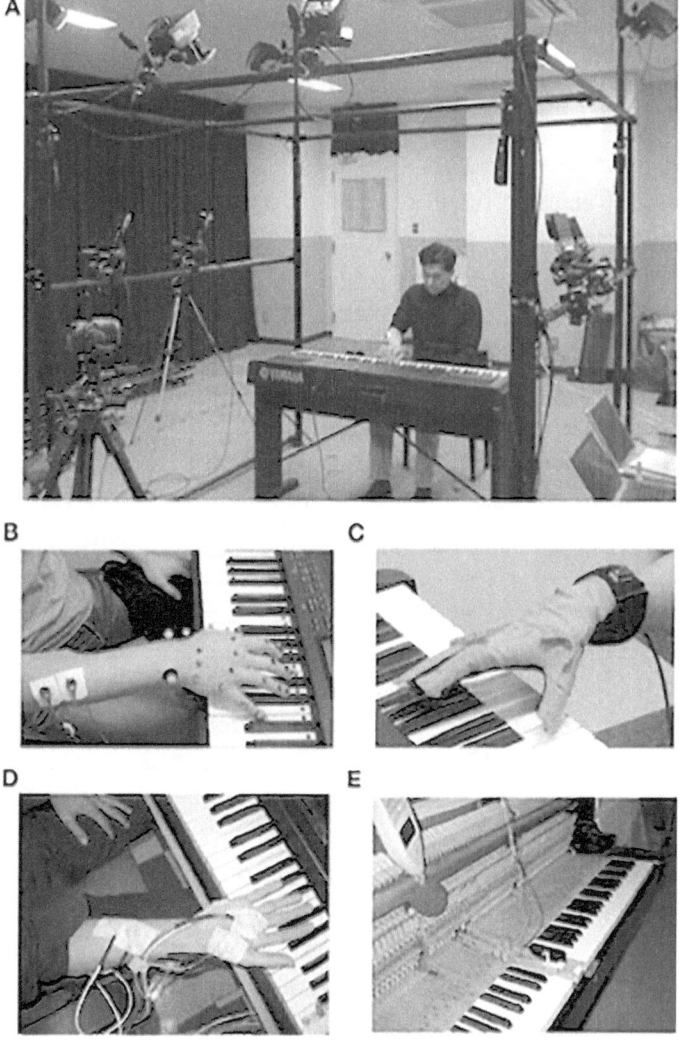

Figure 1: Devices used in past studies to measure the kinematics of piano performance. (A) and (B) are passive systems whereas (C), (D), and (E) are active. (A) displays a motion capture system with high-speed cameras, (B) displays reflective markers, (C) displays a data glove, (D) displays electromyography, and (E) displays a force sensor that is embedded on the piano key (Furuya & Altenmüller, 2013).

Motion Generated by a Touch

Piano touch is the interaction between the pianist and the instrument (MacRitchie, 2015). It is a set of physical parameters used in key depression such as posture, movement, speed, force, and pressure, also including expressive intentions. A cluster of studies have analyzed piano touch, defining it using two categories: struck and press touch. "Struck touch" involves a piano key being pressed by a moving finger whereas "pressed touch" involves a key being pressed by a resting finger.

The repetitive application of these touches produces a force that is a primary cause of musculoskeletal diseases. A 2007 study using a force transducer found that peak angular velocity during wrist flexion (the action of bending the wrist toward the palm) was similar during both types of touch (Kinoshita et al., 2007). However, the angle with which the finger attacked the key was smaller for pressed touch, resulting in increased finger joint extension. It was determined that pressed touch relied heavily on distal muscles, particularly at higher volumes when compared to struck touch. This increased reliance is inefficient; the struck touch is a possible contributor to overuse injuries in pianists.

Another 2013 study found that wrist supination/pronation alongside flexion/extension were stable in pianists (Goebl & Palmer, 2013). Instead, it was the finger joints that experienced a larger range of motion when measuring touch movement. Additionally, the study concluded that slower tempi result in pianists using both struck and pressed touch as opposed to just one.

Skilled vs. Unskilled Musicians

Piano training influences technique and movement when playing. Another cluster of studies have compared the kinematics of novice and professional pianists (MacRitchie, 2015). One study compared differences in tremolo (rapid alternation between notes that result in a shivering/shaking musical effect). Results established that professional pianists reduced muscular load when lifting non-striking fingers when compared to novices. The extension angles of the non-striking fingers were also smaller. However, muscular torque at the metacarpophalangeal joint, wrist, and elbow increased in professional players when compared to novices.

A 1989 study differentiated novice and professional pianists when playing staccato (short and detached) and legato (smooth and connected) notes. Few deviations were noted in finger forces across the various keys. An equation using parameters that measured the force exerted on a key at a given velocity suggested that different techniques can optimize movements, placing less stress on the body and using less force to achieve the same result.

Another 2007 study using LED position sensors attempted to separate movements that are necessary and extraneous when playing the piano. This was done as extraneous movements increase the risk of injury. The study found that professionals used a greater amount of kinetic energy that was "useful" in a keypress compared to novices. There was no difference in total kinetic energy used among the two groups.

Individual Differences in Movement

There are inherent differences in the kinematic profiles of pianists due to the shape of the limbs and the high number of DOF in the hand (MacRitchie, 2015). A 2011 study by Dalla Bella and Palmer determined variations in finger height velocity and acceleration in four professional pianists. There were variations in velocity across all arm joints in eighteen pianists according to a 2012 study. Interestingly, in another 2011 study, the joint motions of five professional pianists playing 30 musical excerpts were recorded in order to determine patterns of covariation in human hand movement (Furuya et al.,

2011). Separate patterns of joint movement were indicated. For instance, a thumb-under maneuver revealed two clusters of movement due to either a right or left translation of the hand along the piano. The thumb-joint velocities were different when comparing the two clusters, but the motions were similar. Moreover, when analyzing a keystroke performed by one finger, three distinct joint rotation patterns were noted. The motion of the striking finger was unvarying between pianists. The motion of the non-striking fingers demonstrated increased variability.

Future Directions

The repository of research on the kinematics associated with musical performance continues to grow. Advancements in devices and systems which can be used to provide quantitative measurement are one aspect of this growth. Past studies have identified various properties and kinematic analysis. In the future, it is important to delve deeper into the variety of movements that result in a musical outcome (e.x. piano touch). This can aid musicians to apply minute postural and movement changes which prevent injury. Albeit, the DOF problem and sheer complexity of the human anatomy present a challenge in this inquiry.

Works Cited

Chiaverini, S., Oriolo, G., & Walker, I. D. (2008). Kinematically Redundant Manipulators. In B. Siciliano & O. Khatib (Eds.), Springer Handbook of Robotics (pp. 245–268). Springer Berlin Heidelberg. https://doi.org/10.1007/978-3-540-30301-5_12

Cluss, M., Laws, K., Martin, N., Nowicki, T. S., & Mira, A. (2006). The indirect measurement of biomechanical forces in the moving human body. American Journal of Physics, 74(2), 102–108. https://doi.org/10.1119/1.2149868

ElKoura, G., & Singh, K. (n.d.). Handrix: Animating the Human Hand. 11.

Furuya, S., & Altenmüller, E. (2013). Flexibility of movement organization in piano performance. Frontiers in Human Neuroscience, 7. https://doi.org/10.3389/fnhum.2013.00173

Furuya, S., Flanders, M., & Soechting, J. F. (2011). Hand kinematics of piano playing. Journal of Neurophysiology, 106(6), 2849–2864. https://doi.org/10.1152/jn.00378.2011

Goebl, W., & Palmer, C. (2013). Temporal Control and Hand Movement Efficiency in Skilled Music Performance. PloS One, 8, e50901. https://doi.org/10.1371/journal.pone.0050901

Kinoshita, H., Furuya, S., Aoki, T., & Altenmüller, E. (2007). Loudness control in pianists as exemplified in keystroke force measurements on different touches. The Journal of the Acoustical Society of America, 121(5), 2959. https://doi.org/10.1121/1.2717493

MacRitchie, J. (2015). The art and science behind piano touch: A review connecting multi-disciplinary literature. Musicae Scientiae, 19(2), 171–190. https://doi.org/10.1177/1029864915572813

Morasso, P. (2022). A Vexing Question in Motor Control: The Degrees of Freedom Problem. Frontiers in Bioengineering and Biotechnology, 9, 783501. https://doi.org/10.3389/fbioe.2021.783501

Russell, D. L. (n.d.). Establishing a Biomechanical Basis for Injury Preventative Piano Pedagogy. 13.

Todd, N. P. M. (1995). The kinematics of musical expression. The Journal of the Acoustical Society of America, 97(3), 1940–1949. https://doi.org/10.1121/1.412067

Wristen, B. G. (2000). Avoiding Piano-related Injury: A Proposed Theoretical Procedure for Biomechanical Analysis of Piano Technique. Medical Problems of Performing Artists, 15(2), 55–64. https://doi.org/10.21091/mppa.2000.2012

CHAPTER TWO

Neuromechanics/Neurology of Music in Respect to Piano and Violin

By: Laiyba Wasim

Introduction

Neuromechanics is a branch of movement science that describes the interactive relationship between the brain, muscles, and sense organs in a stable and dynamic environment (Nishikawa et al., 2007). In the past, the study of motor control has only been analyzed relative to neuroscience, while the role of body mechanics has been downplayed (Nishikawa et al., 2007). But now as more insight is gained about the motor control in the human body, this is no longer the case (Nishikawa et al., 2007).

Music involves the integration of three major modalities; the motor information, multimodal sensory information and the auditory feedback system to produced sophisticated movements (Altenmüller, 2008). These sophisticated motor movements require considerable effort and time (Anat, 2007; Altenmüller, 2008). The brain has adapted both structurally and functionally in response to these motor movements (Altenmüller, 2008). However, these motor movement can deteriorate along with the central and autonomic nervous system, causing focal dystonia (Niu, 2020). The chapter will talk about the motor and sensory pathways of the brain, the structural and functional plasticity adaptations, and the curse of focal dystonia, as they relate to pianists and violinists.

Music: A Product of Sensory and Motor Pathways in the Brain

As mentioned above, learning a musical instrument involves the interaction of both, cognition and modalities (Herholz and Zatorre, 2012). They work together to produce structural, functional, and behavioural changes that may take from days to perhaps years (Herholz and Zatorre, 2012). Whether one is a pianist or violinist, they follow the same general pathway described below. We will begin the pathway with the vestibulospinal and reticulospinal tracts.

In the brain stem, the vestibulospinal and reticulospinal tracts help the musician keep the appropriate posture of the trunk and shoulder girdle by not only steadying the upper limbs, but also ensuring the flexible control of wrist and fingers (Metcalf et al., 2014). The motor activity needed to perform originates within the motor cortices that include the cerebellum and basal ganglia, and they give rise to the voluntary and autonomic movements (Metcalf et al., 2014). It is important to note that the primary motor cortex contains the somatotopic map of the body (Anat, 2007). The pyramidal cells within this map are basically involved in the control of hands, upper limbs, lower limbs, trunk and face muscles (Anat, 2007). These branches of these axons end up in the motor pools of the body, which may lie in the segments of our spine (Anat, 2007). The electrical stimulation produced from the primary motor cortex then produce the well-coordinated movement required (Anat, 2007). During this process, the cerebellum is accomplishing its own role. It is combining the visual, proprioceptive, vestibular and tactile sensory information, which it can then use to modify the trajectory of the movements the musician is undergoing (Metcalf et al., 2014). This modification is undertaken through the descending neural pathways, one of them being the corticospinal tract (Metcalf et al., 2014).

Next, the signals generated from the motor context, travel from the upper motor neurones and end up terminating on the anterior horn cells in the spinal cord (Metcalf et al., 2014). Action potentials are generated here now, which travel through the lower motor neurons (Metcalf et al., 2014). They synapse and generate a contraction in the muscle (Metcalf et al., 2014). The contraction varies in strength due to the spatial and temporal summation of the activated lower motor neuron (Metcalf et al., 2014).

We also need to understand that the neuromechanics of a beginner and a professional in music differs. When a person first learns a new set of movement, the presupplementary area becomes active but only for a limited period of time (Anat, 2007). The supplementary motor cortex, an area posterior to the presupplementary area, shows even less of an activity during the learning phase, but once the movement is learned, it becomes active (Anat, 2007). The premotor cortex is also extremely active during the learning phase (Anat, 2007). Once the set of movement is learned and its sequence becomes automatic, the situation changes completely (Anat, 2007). Now the activation in the premotor cortex decreases, while activity increases within the primary motor cortex (Anat, 2007). The activity is maintained within the supplementary cortex (Anat, 2007). Movements that have become automatic will be performed much more rapidly compared to new muscle movements (Smith, 1887). The signals to carry out these automatic movements travel from the brain to the automatic system in the nerve centres. These centres then carry the stimulus to the extensor and flexor finger muscles, which triggers their contraction (Smith, 1887). The rate of finger contraction varies from person to person and can be measured by the number of notes from a new sequence that one can play within a second (Smith, 1887).

Music: Stimulus for Brain Plasticity in the Context of Musicians (Pianists and Violinists) and Non-Musicians

Because music has become a major issue within the field of cognitive neuroscience, its role associated with the structural and functional plasticity of the brain has become an area of research (Jäncke, 2009). This structural and functional plasticity is a result of the motor and cognitive abilities required when playing a musical instrument (Johansson, 2006). Plasticity is defined as the "general ability of the central nervous system to adapt to changing environmental conditions and newly imposed tasks during its entire lifespan" (Altenmüller, 2008).

Structural Plasticity

Let us analyze the role of music in the structural plasticity of brain, which has become more apparent thanks to the brain imaging that has become available to us.

First, research conducted by Bangert et al., 2006 compared the "omega sign," of the precentral gyrus between the pianists and the violinists. The omega sign is indicative of a larger hand motor area (Schlaug, 2015; Jäncke, 2009). The results showed that pianist had the omega sign on both hemispheres, which was likely because they utilize both hands during playing (Schlaug, 2015; Jäncke, 2009). On the other hand, the violinists only showed the omega sign on their right hemisphere, which corresponds to the left hand (Schlaug, 2015; Jäncke, 2009), the hand more frequently in use while holding the bow and manipulating the strings playing (Jäncke, 2009). This adaptation was more prominent in instrumentalist who started to play before the age of ten and had extensive experience in this field (Altenmüller, 2008).

Another study noted similar results with respect to the size and specialization of the corpus callosum (Altenmüller, 2008). The anterior portion of the corpus callosum was larger in size for professional violinists and pianists who had started before the age of seven (Altenmüller, 2008). The anterior portion contains fibres from the supplementary motor areas and motor areas (Altenmüller, 2008). Because playing musical instruments require the coordination of both hands, the fibres get stimulated more, resulting in their myelination and prevention of aging (Altenmüller, 2008). However, one difference noted through the magnetoencephalography was that in violinists, the sensory areas, which correspond to the second to fifth finger on the left hand, were enlarged compared to non-musicians (Altenmüller, 2008).

Lastly, a regression study conducted by Groussard et al., 2014, compared the grey matter tracts in the left hippocampus, right middle and superior frontal regions, right insula, supplementary motor area, left superior temporal lobe and posterior cingulate areas of amateur musicians that could play one or more instruments such as the piano and the violin, and the non-musicians. Groussard et al., 2014 discovered that engaging in musical practice resulted in a noticeable change in grey matter, which was most obvious in the expert musician groups, then the intermediate, and last, the non-musicians. These changes occurred in the left hippocampus, superior frontal and right middle regions of the brain (Groussard et al., 2014). After years of practice, changes within the right supplementary motor areas, and the left superior temporal and posterior cingulate appeared as well and with the same pattern (Groussard et al., 2014).

Through these examples mentioned above, it is obvious that playing musical instrument(s) can cause dynamic structural changes within the brain.

Functional Plasticity

Playing musical instruments have also resulted in the development of functional plasticity in the brain. A study mentioned by Schlaug, 2015 in his paper, "Musicians and music making as a model for the study of brain plasticity" explains that the somatosensory representations of the fingers involved in the playing of string instruments were larger compared to those of non-musicians (Schlaug, 2015). This was specially the case for the fifth finger, which is barely used by non-musicians (Schlaug, 2015). Those who had been playing before the age of thirteen has the largest cortical representation of the fifth finger compared to those who started later, while those that started later had larger representations in comparison to the non-musicians (Schlaug, 2015). Pantev et al., 1998 also obtained similar results in their study, that those who played earlier in their lives had the greatest representations (Herholz and Zatorre, 2012). However, it was interesting to note that the enlarged representation observed was purely for piano tones in pianists, while violinists showed larger cortical response solely to violin sounds (Schlaug, 2015). However, this distinction of sounds was not observed with non-musicians (Schlaug, 2015).

Another study looked at the involvement of sensorimotor and auditory system for instrumentalists (Herholz and Zatorre, 2012). Herholz and Zatorre, 2012 proved that plasticity depends upon experience with the instruments. For instance, Pantev et al., 1998 discovered that those who practiced the piano had enlarged auditory cortical evoked potentials, while the fMRI results of a study conducted by Margulis et al., 2009 on violinists and flutists had the same results but this time with precentral and inferior frontal areas, both which are involved in the syntax processing and auditory-motor interactions (Herholz and Zatorre, 2012).

Rüber et al. 2013 also assessed the corticospinal motor tracts of keyboard players, string players and non-musicians (Schlaug, 2015).. The FA values for the motor tracts within the left hemisphere were greatest in keyboard players, while they were high in the right hemisphere for both musician groups (Schlaug, 2015). They also measured the white matter tracts within the right motor cortex and understood that the differences were a result of the tapping rate of the index fingers across the groups involved (Schlaug, 2015). The difference revealed that the adaption could have been the result of the different motor demands of the different musical instruments (Schlaug, 2015).

Moreover, Elbert et al. (1995) studied the left and right lateralization of the hemispheres that were responsible for the motor control of the musical instruments (Herholz and Zatorre, 2012). They discovered that through the measurement of tactile evoked responses measured in MEG, the cortical representation of the fingers of left hands were expanded compared to their right hands (Herholz and Zatorre, 2012). The left hands were involved in the tuning of the strings during playing (Herholz and Zatorre, 2012).

Through these studies, it is quite obvious that music, a mechanical stimulator, has an ever-lasting impact on the nervous system of individuals (Azizi, 2009). Learning to play musical instruments, such as the piano and the violin, has been used to study for the structural and functional neuroplasticity of the brain (Reybrouck et al., 2017). This neuroplasticity starts earlier in life since the brain is known to be more sensitive to plastic changes at this point in time (Reybrouck et al., 2017). Then these plasticity changes continue throughout life (Reybrouck et al., 2017). They include various systems of the body, including motor planning, preparation and execution, as well as the numerous sensory modalities, some of which have been discussed in the above-mentioned examples (Reybrouck et al., 2017).

Music: The curse of Dystonia

Along with the specialization of brain structures that come with music performances, there appears a dark side of the loss of skilled hand movements (Altenmüller, 2008). This degradation of movement is referred to as focal dystonia or musician's dystonia (Altenmüller and Jabusch, 2010). Altenmüller and Jabusch, 2010 define it as a "motor disorder consisting of involuntary sustained muscle contractions that interfere with the voluntary motor control during the play of a musical instrument." About one out of hundred professional musicians suffer this disorder, and, the majority of the time, it ends their career. (Altenmüller, 2008)

The pathophysiology of focal dystonia has not yet been clearly discovered (Altenmüller and Jabusch, 2010). However, several findings include the following:

- Maladaptive plasticity (Altenmüller and Jabusch, 2010)

- Changes in the sensorimotor processing (Altenmüller and Jabusch, 2010)

- Reduction in the inhibition of central nervous system (Altenmüller and Jabusch, 2010)

Focal Dystonia often appears to be painless, and symptoms gradually become severe (Anat, 2007). A musician's fingers may feel heavy (Anat, 2007), experience irregular trills or involuntary flexion and then eventually become incapacitated (Konczek and Abbruzzese, 2013).

The loss of muscle control is often seen in pianists as a coactivation of both the extensor and flexor wrist muscles (Konczek and Abbruzzese, 2013). There is a co-contraction of antagonistic muscle groups (Konczek and Abbruzzese, 2013). Once the condition advances, the fingers then begin to go through hyperflexion, and the pianist's nail instead touches the key and not the pad (Anat, 2007). In the other scenario, the fingers cannot be brough down to the string or key (Anat, 2007). In the later stages, the frequent contractions occurring between antagonist flexor and extensor muscles of the digits causes pain and exhaustion (Anat, 2007).

It is also important to know that musicians who play, for instance, the piano and violin, may only experience dystonia for one instrument (Anat, 2007). In pianists, seventy percent of the time, it is the right hand that suffers from dystonia, while in violinists, three-fourths of the time, it is the left hand that experiences dystonia (Anat, 2007).

Dystonia can be treated through pharmacological interventions (trihexyphenidyl or botulinum toxin-A), ergonomic changes in the instrument, and retraining programs. However, only a minority of affected musicians can recover their motor control (Altenmüller and Jabusch, 2010).

Conclusion

In summary, one way to study the neuroplasticity of the brain is to study the effects of musical performance on the auditory and the sensorimotor domains (Altenmüller, 2008). There is clear evidence that music causes plastic changes within the central nervous system, both structurally and functionally (Altenmüller, 2008). However, it can also lead to focal dystonia (Altenmüller, 2008).

Works Cited

Altenmüller E. (2008). Neurology of musical performance. Clinical medicine (London, England), 8(4), 410–413. https://doi.org/10.7861/clinmedicine.8-4-410

Altenmüller, E., & Jabusch, H. C. (2010). Focal dystonia in musicians: phenomenology, pathophysiology and triggering factors. European journal of neurology, 17 Suppl 1, 31–36. https://doi.org/10.1111/j.1468-1331.2010.03048.x

Azizi S. A. (2009). Brain to music to brain!. Neuroscience letters, 459(1), 1–2. https://doi.org/10.1016/j.neulet.2009.04.038

Groussard, M., Viader, F., Landeau, B., Desgranges, B., Eustache, F., & Platel, H. (2014). The effects of musical practice on structural plasticity: the dynamics of grey matter changes. Brain and cognition, 90, 174–180. https://doi.org/10.1016/j.bandc.2014.06.013

Herholz, S. C., & Zatorre, R. J. (2012). Musical training as a framework for brain plasticity: behavior, function, and structure. Neuron, 76(3), 486–502. https://doi.org/10.1016/j.neuron.2012.10.011

Jäncke L. (2009). Music drives brain plasticity. F1000 biology reports, 1, 78. https://doi.org/10.3410/B1-78

JOHANSSON, B. A. R. B. R. O. B. (2006). Music and brain plasticity. European Review, 14(1), 49–64. http://doi.org/10.1017/S1062798706000056

Konczak, J., & Abbruzzese, G. (2013). Focal dystonia in musicians: linking motor symptoms to somatosensory dysfunction. Frontiers in human neuroscience, 7, 297. https://doi.org/10.3389/fnhum.2013.00297

Metcalf, C. D., Irvine, T. A., Sims, J. L., Wang, Y. L., Su, A. W., & Norris, D. O. (2014). Complex hand dexterity: a review of biomechanical methods for measuring musical performance. Frontiers in psychology, 5, 414. https://doi.org/10.3389/fpsyg.2014.00414

Nishikawa, K., Biewener, A. A., Aerts, P., Anna N. Ahn, Chiel, H. J., Daley, M. A., Daniel, T. L., Full, R. J., Hale, M. E., Hedrick, T.

L., Lappin, A. K., Nichols, T. R., Quinn, R. D., Satterlie, R. A., & Brett Szymik. (2007). Neuromechanics: An Integrative Approach for Understanding Motor Control. Integrative and Comparative Biology, 47(1), 16–54. http://www.jstor.org/stable/4540133

Niu, Ruixi, "Types and Causes of Physiological Injury in Piano Playing, with Emphasis on Piano Pedagogy in China" (2020). Graduate Theses, Dissertations, and Problem Reports. 7693. https://researchrepository.wvu.edu/etd/7693

Reybrouck, M., Vuust, P., & Brattico, E. (2018). Music and Brain Plasticity: How Sounds Trigger Neurogenerative Adaptations. In (Ed.), Neuroplasticity - Insights of Neural Reorganization. IntechOpen. https://doi.org/10.5772/intechopen.74318

Schlaug G. (2015). Musicians and music making as a model for the study of brain plasticity. Progress in brain research, 217, 37–55. https://doi.org/10.1016/bs.pbr.2014.11.020

Smith, W. M. (1887). The Physiology of Pianoforte Playing, with a Practical Application of a New Theory. Proceedings of the Musical Association, 14, 43–66. http://www.jstor.org/stable/765394

Watson A. H. (2006). What can studying musicians tell us about motor control of the hand?. Journal of anatomy, 208(4), 527–542. https://doi.org/10.1111/j.1469-7580.2006.00545.x

CHAPTER THREE

Music Therapy: Introduction and Popularization of Music in Clinical Healthcare Settings

By: HanShu

What could recondition a soldier who has seen the worst of humanity, reliving the terrors of his comrades gassed and blown up into fragments? The same sounds their expectant mothers played for them while inhabited in the womb – music. Described as a forever illustrious part of human history, music continuously proves to be a pivotal component of one's well-being and a raw reflection of the human experience.

Ancient musical rituals could be inferred as a prehistoric form of religion – drums, chants, and flutes craved in bones – to invoke individuation (Conrad, 2010). Egyptian medical papyri writing describes music being used to influence the human body. Mythological and biblical written works, as well as Greco-Roman, Arabian, Indian, and Chinese traditional medical teachings include various notions of music used in a therapeutic way (Gracida, 2018).

The great Greek philosophers Plato and his student Aristotle had differing views on music; but agreed that music was to either (1) move or imitate emotions, (2) give pleasure, (3) dispose of moral virtue, or (4) foster intellectual advancement (Gracida, 2018).

During the European Middle Ages, the law mandated aspiring physicians to be appreciative of music, due to beliefs that music healed the psyche and the body (Conrad, 2010). The late 19th century saw experiments led by Herman von Helmholtz involving investigations into the emotional effects of harmonies on the human psyche using an excitable tuning fork, paving the road for the application of music in clinical settings (Conrad, 2010).

Early documented cases within modern medicine showed the effect of musical interventions during surgical procedures. For instance, doctors after the 1877 invention of the phonograph played music as a sedative or distraction in the operating room (Gracida, 2018). Frederick Harford recruited a choir to play for patients at various London hospitals (Gracida, 2018).

Post-Colonization North American roots of music therapy began during the American Civil War when musicians played for injured soldiers. This continued throughout the world wars, where music was purposed to entertain and build morale amongst armed forces members (Gracida, 2018).

After WW2, community musicians performed for those coping with war-related physical and emotional trauma. Along with the wounded soldiers' consistent and positive responses to music, the U.S. War Department's 1945 Technical Bulletin detailed a program incorporating music in traditional therapeutic services, such as recreation, education, occupational and physical reconditing for service members convalescing (American Music Therapy Association, n.d.). Research and endorsement of the Army and Office of the Surgeon General post-WW2 is said to be a father of the modern music therapy profession.

In the present day, music therapy is defined as the "clinical, evidence-based use of music interventions to accomplish individualized goals within a therapeutic relationship". Instead of casual music listening, music therapists utilize unique qualities, such as the tempo, dynamics, and rhythm, to access a patient's emotions and memories, and address an immediate response based on their needs. (American Music Therapy Association, n.d; de Witte et al., 2020).

TikTok videos of concertgoers in tears over English singer and songwriter's live performances of Fine Line and Matilda, young children being enrolled by their parents to learn instruments, and the influx of tech giants investing in the music industry prove music perfectly encapsulates humility and betters one's emotions even in the twenty-first century.

Cerebral Palsy:

Cerebral palsy, a disorder affecting the development of movements and postures, adds limitations on activity and is attributed to non-progressive disturbances occurring in a fetus' or infant's brain. The motor disorder is often in combination with alterations to a child's lifelong sensation, perception, cognitive, and communicative abilities as a consequence of epilepsy and secondary musculoskeletal concerns (Schulzne, 2022).

The traditional physical therapy approach, incorporated with music therapy, could be a great advantage to Cerebral Palsy (CP) patients to enhance motor functions through an easier execution of voluntary movements. Patients, despite limited motor function, could integrate the use of rhythm and movement and musical instruments into physiotherapy, benefiting neuroplasticity and motor control (Vinolo-Gil et al, 2021). Starting in the 1990s, there are some well-documented cases of music therapy used amongst CP patients to influence muscle tone as tight and stiff muscles cause difficulty in controlling movement. Amongst individuals living with CP, if the lower body muscles are overly toned, impaired walking may result in a "jerky, awkward gait" (Schulzne, 2022; Vinolo-Gil et al., 2021).

Vinolo-Gil et al. (2021)'s clinical study involved hearing CP patients of any age with the ability to perceive verbal instructions and ability to plan and carry out voluntary movements. Types of interventions included a drum to emphasize the cadence and using chord progressions on a keyboard to play a simple rhythm pattern (Vinolo-Gil et al., 2021). The results showed that there was evidence of the benefits of combined music and physical therapy in improving patients' motor function but a larger sample group and more specific criteria for measuring motor function are required (Vinolo-Gil et al., 2021). Vinolo-Gil et al.'s particular study analyzed the patient's strides' length, velocity, symmetry, cadence, step length, knee extension power, balance, upper limb position, and locomotor stages.

Postoperative Pain:

American national guidelines for post-operative pain management describe many patients to have uncontrolled pain that could slow wound healing and lead to anxiety and depression; with more than 80% of post-op patients experiencing moderate-to-severe pain (Tse et al., 2005; Whitaker, 2010).

Unrelieved pain activates one's sympathetic nervous system, which could be destructive to their cardiovascular, gastrointestinal, and renal systems; thus, predisposing them to fatal yet preventable complications, such as cardiac ischemia, decreased blood flow and oxygen to the heart. Moreover, pain could inhibit movement and resilience (Whitaker, 2010).

Compelling evidence, through randomized controlled trials, exists that music therapy serves to be an accessible, cost-effective, and benign intervention to reduce postoperative pain (Locsin, 1981). Results from patients undergoing nasal or gynecologic surgery, or open coronary artery bypass grafting demonstrate that music therapy has the potential to promote relaxation through psychological effects, and an increased oxytocin release. Oxytocin, also known as the love hormone, is produced in the brain's hypothalamus and released to be circulated by the pituitary gland (Whitaker, 2010). It is released in response to stress and creates a sense of calmness, diminishes the sensation of pain, and promotes wound healing, like the effects of oxytocin during childbirth and the postpartum period. Increasingly lower levels of oxytocin have been associated with more pain and anxiousness (Nilsson, 2009; Whitaker, 2010).

Current studies had patients partaking in 30-minute sessions, but further research is required to determine the most effective duration and frequency of music therapy. The possibility of repeated sessions and the influences of different music genres on the human innate stress response could be considered (Whitaker, 2010).

Moreover, infection control is vital in all operative settings, including recovery. No amount of Ludwig van Beethoven could counteract bacteria-induced post-surgical complications, including green bloody mucus and discharge oozing from the surgical site (Whitaker, 2010). Caregivers must consider the risk posed by sharing equipment such as headphones.

The aforementioned complications would result in a longer hospitalization and recovery, benefiting the deep pockets of hospital investors but robbing one's child of quintessential extracurricular activities and putting their family in debt.

Stress and Depression:

Depression, a recognized chronic disease, has become more prevalent amongst adolescents. Often resulting in a loss of social function and consequently lower quality of life and increased mortality; fortunately, music intervention is possible and evidently effective.

Stress amongst Americans has been deemed a national mental health crisis - where Gen Z'ers are particularly vulnerable to the potential long-term consequences of persistent stress. They faced unprecedented uncertainty and had reported symptoms of depression, in the American Psychological Association (APA)'s annual Stress in America survey. Two years and counting since COVID-19 was declared a pandemic serves no help, as a hefty amalgam of stressors has significant consequences on all minds and bodies (APA, 2020). In the same survey, older adults were described to have embraced the "this, too, shall pass" mentality. Gen Z adolescent's prominent stressors, including a rise in suicide rates, almost normalized sexual assault reports, stripping of women's rights, and racialized violence, negatively impact their motivation and concentration and participation in extracurriculars. Moreover, declines in social interaction and closeness with relationships were reported (APA, 2020).

Furthermore, environmental factors, including the COVID-19 pandemic and recent political instability, trigger an adaptive response to stress (APA, 2020). Prolonged and excessive stress without effective coping strategies may lead to maladaptive changes, which in turn may contribute to the development of pathological conditions such as anxiety and mood disorders, including depression, especially amongst those with increased genetic vulnerability (Tafet & Nemeroff, 2016).

Unlike tranquilizing prescriptions, with negative contraindications such as substance misuse disorder, music therapy, being a non-pharmacological therapeutic intervention could prove to be especially beneficial. Music listening, without the presence of a trained music therapist, is strongly associated with a decrease in stress due to the reduction of physiological arousal marked by reduced cortisol levels, lowered heart rate, and decreases in mean arterial pressure (de Witte et al., 2020). Certain music can also reduce negative emotions and feelings, where the symptoms include subjective worry, state anxiety, restlessness, or nervousness. Brain structures, in particular the amygdala and mesolimbic reward system are involved in emotional and motivational processes is modulated by music and could enhance one's resilience (Tafet & Nemeroff; 2016; de Witte et al., 2020).

Health-related Music Listening and Digitalized Medicine:

The invention of the internet and the rising popularity of digital medicine has healthcare practices shifting away from the traditional one-size-fits-all approach to clearing as many beds as possible in the overcrowded and understaffed Emergency Department. Instead, patients crave convenience and favour personalized medicine and non-pharmaceutical health solutions (Fitzpatrick, 2021). Despite that, music still plays an integral part in healthcare.

Streaming services, such as Spotify; are contributing to a future incorporating music into everyday wellness. With recent patents filed to strengthen their services, they plan on engineering more personalized music recommendations for wellness outcomes (Fitzpatrick, 2021).

Apple, with its music streaming service, is influential in how twenty-first-century life. Their Apple Watch sales and focus on updates to the Health app within iOS updates show the trend the healthcare industry is advancing in. Especially with the popularity of listening to music to enhance one's health, Apple has begun to integrate music features into their platform and is investing in music and wellness tech start-ups (Fitzpatrick, 2021).

Community-based Music Interventions:

Increasing numbers of women involved in the war effort, as civilian or military personnel, can be correlated with music being used to enhance the well-being of the troops.; acting in a way like the beloved American cultural icon—Rosie the Riveter.

Eighty yeara later, music is still purposed to address inequities. Caló et al. (2020) discuss music-based intervention as a public health tool in recent years to enhance positive health outcomes for young people in Scotland. Health policies focused on social inclusion have recognized adolescents' participation in creative arts as it promoted social connectedness and self-esteem amongst the disadvantaged in youth custodial and community settings (Caló et al., 2020).

The majority of the aforementioned musical interventions for health concerns involved listening to music. However, Heavy Sound, a Scottish-based organization, engages youth from deprived communities and with numerous adverse childhood experiences by running participatory music-making sessions for them to express repressed emotions. Through voluntary questionnaires – structured using the Good Childhood Index and life satisfaction measures of personal well-being by the ONS National Wellbeing Programme – the participants reported increasing self-confidence and a state of well-being. Feeling safe was a common trigger but with the achievement of trust and connectedness reinforced by the music space, adolescent participants felt nurtured, protected, and fulfilled (Caló et al., 2020). Their positive feelings of togetherness and bonding leads to the release of endorphin and oxytocin neurotransmitters, both enhancing an individual's defensive response to stress (de Witte et al., 2020).

Like all else, the COVID-19 pandemic has played a role in shaping the significance of music in the lives of people in the twenty-first century (Fitzpatrick, 2021; Martínez-Castilla et al., 2021). A 2020 study in Spain during one of the nation's strictest lockdowns revealed music to have contributed to enhancing one's well-being, counteracting negative emotions brought on because of the public health crisis. Italian healthcare staff facing an unknown, yet fatal illness proved music to be of great benefit as findings showed that it enhanced emotional well-being by reducing feelings of fear, sadness, and worry (Martínez-Castilla et al., 2021).

Future of Music Therapy and Final Thoughts:

The development and popularized use of music, includes addressing a patient's physical, emotional, cognitive, and social needs through a therapeutic relationship and becoming a central treatment modality in rehabilitation. The American Music Therapy Association represents 6000+ members and regulates the rising health profession (American Music Therapy Association, n.d.).

Neurobiological studies have intrinsically connected music to a role in bettering and shaping brain function. Current research focuses on the brain's apparent exercise-dependent plasticity and music's profound influence on learning, cognitive development, and recovery of function (Thaut, 2005). Findings include the rhythmic entrainment of motor function where music acts as sensory timers that sequences and the coordination of movement, similar to a military marching band, could aid in movement restoration in stroke, Parkinson's, or traumatic brain injury patients (Thaut, 2005).

Numerous clinical studies were strikingly evident in concluding that auditory rhythm and music should be effectively adapted for specific therapeutic purposes. Music therapy is shifting from the traditional social science model built on cultural roles and well-being practices to a neuroscience discipline drawing from brain function and music perception (American Music Therapy Association, n.d.; Thaut, 2005).

Like all else, the COVID-19 pandemic has played a role in shaping the significance of music within the lives of people in the twenty-first century (Fitzpatrick, 2021; Martínez-Castilla et al., 2021). A 2020 study in Spain during one of the nation's strictest lockdowns revealed music to have contributed to enhancing one's well-being, counteracting negative emotions brought on because of the public health crisis. Italian healthcare staff facing an unknown, yet fatal illness proved music to be of great benefit as findings showed that it enhanced emotional wellbeing by reducing feelings of fear, sadness, and worry (Martínez-Castilla et al., 2021).

Like all else, the COVID-19 pandemic has played a role in shaping the significance of music in the lives of people in the twenty-first century (Fitzpatrick, 2021; Martínez-Castilla et al., 2021). A 2020 study in Spain during one of the nation's strictest lockdowns revealed music to have contributed to enhancing well-being by counteracting negative emotions brought on by the public health crisis. Italian healthcare staff facing an unknown, yet fatal illness indicated music to be of great benefit as findings showed that it enhanced emotional well-being by reducing feelings of fear, sadness, and worry (Martínez-Castilla et al., 2021).

Medicine is the perfect marriage of the arts and sciences, present in many parts of the world since antiquity, incorporating biological mechanisms to devising a humane approach to pain after making sense of sickness and suffering. Perceptions of the role of music in medicine evolved from a supportive role to foster relationships and emotional expression to brain imaging scans documenting a melody's physiological effects.

Using music within the health sciences bridges the gap between the arts and sciences, where music therapy has become a widely recognized and respected evidence-based rehabilitation discipline.

Works Cited

About Music Therapy & AMTA. American Music Therapy Association . (n.d.). Retrieved July 5, 2022, from https://www.musictherapy.org/about/

American Psychological Association. (2020, October). Stress in America™ 2020: A National Mental Health Crisis. American Psychological Association. Retrieved July 2, 2022, from https://www.apa.org/news/press/releases/stress/2020/report-october

Caló, F., Steiner, A., Millar, S., & Teasdale, S. (2020). The impact of a community-based music intervention on the health and well-being of young people: A realist evaluation. Health & Social Care in the Community, 28(3), 988–997. https://doi.org/10.1111/hsc.12931

Conrad, C. (2010). Music for Healing: From Magic to Medicine. The Lancet, 376(9757), 1980–1981. https://doi.org/10.1016/s0140-6736(10)62251-9

de Witte, M., da Silva Pinho, A., Stams, G.-J., Moonen, X., Bos, A. E. R., & van Hooren, S. (2020). Music Therapy for Stress Reduction: A Systematic Review and Meta-Analysis. Health Psychology Review, 16(1), 134–159. https://doi.org/10.1080/17437199.2020.1846580

Fitzpatrick, F. (2021, August 25). Could Music Be A Game-Changer For The Future of Digital Health? Forbes. Retrieved July 2, 2022, from https://www.forbes.com/sites/frankfitzpatrick/2021/08/25/could-music-be-a-game-changer-for-the-future-of-digital-health/?sh=1248028970c7

Gracida, L. S. (2018, October 8). History of Music Therapy: From Antiquity to Today. Sam's Fans. Retrieved July 2, 2022, from https://samsfans.org/history-music-therapy/#:~:text=It%20was%20during%20both%20World,veterans%20retain%20their%20mental%20health.

Locsin, R. G. (1981). The Effect of Music on the Pain of Selected Post-Operative Patients. Journal of Advanced Nursing, 6(1), 19–25. https://doi.org/10.1111/j.1365-2648.1981.tb03091.x

Martínez-Castilla, P., Gutiérrez-Blasco, I. M., Spitz, D. H., & Granot, R. (2021). The Efficacy of Music for Emotional Wellbeing During the COVID-19 Lockdown in Spain: An Analysis of Personal and Context-Related Variables. Frontiers in Psychology, 12. https://doi.org/10.3389/fpsyg.2021.647837

Minor, L. (2021, April 19). Recognition of the Power of Music in Medicine is Growing. Scope. Retrieved July 2, 2022, from https://scopeblog.stanford.edu/2021/04/20/recognition-of-the-power-of-music-in-medicine-is-growing/#:~:text=Music%20therapy%20has%20proven%20effective,in%20managing%20Alzheimer's%20and%20dementia.

Music Therapy and Military Populations. American Music Therapy Association. (n.d.). Retrieved July 2, 2022, from https://www.musictherapy.org/research/music_therapy_and_military_populations/

Nilsson, U. (2009). Soothing music can increase oxytocin levels during bed rest after open-heart surgery: A randomised control trial. Journal of Clinical Nursing, 18(15), 2153–2161. https://doi.org/10.1111/j.1365-2702.2008.02718.x

Schulzne, S. (2022, April 19). Cerebral Palsy and Mobility Issues. Cerebral Palsy Guidance. Retrieved July 7, 2022, from https://www.cerebralpalsyguidance.com/cerebral-palsy/associated-disorders/mobility-issues/#:~:text=Tight%2C%20stiff%2C%20overly%20toned%20muscles,causes%20a%20jerky%2C%20awkward%20gait.

Tafet, G. E., & Nemeroff, C. B. (2016). The Links Between Stress and Depression: Psychoneuroendocrinological, Genetic, and Environmental Interactions. The Journal of Neuropsychiatry and Clinical Neurosciences, 28(2), 77–88. https://doi.org/10.1176/appi.neuropsych.15030053

Thaut, M. H. (2005). The Future of Music in therapy and medicine. Annals of the New York Academy of Sciences, 1060(1), 303–308. https://doi.org/10.1196/annals.1360.023

Tse, M. M., Chan, M. F., & Benzie, I. F. (2005). The effect of music therapy on postoperative pain, heart rate, systolic blood pressure and analgesic use following nasal surgery. Journal of Pain & Palliative Care Pharmacotherapy, 19(3), 21–29. https://doi.org/10.1080/j354v19n03_05

Universitaet Tuebingen. (2009, June 25). Paleolithic Bone Flute Discovered: Earliest Musical Tradition Documented In Southwestern Germany. ScienceDaily. Retrieved July 2, 2022, from https://www.sciencedaily.com/releases/2009/06/090624213346.htm

Vinolo-Gil, M. J., Casado-Fernández, E., Perez-Cabezas, V., Gonzalez-Medina, G., Martín-Vega, F. J., & Martín-Valero, R. (2021). Effects of the combination of music therapy and physiotherapy in the improvement of motor function in Cerebral Palsy: A challenge for research. Children, 8(10), 868. https://doi.org/10.3390/children8100868

Whitaker, M. H. (2010). Sounds Soothing - Music Therapy for Postoperative Pain. Nursing, 40(12), 53–54. https://doi.org/10.1097/01.nurse.0000390680.80395.cd

Whitfield, S. (2010). Music: Its Expressive Power and Moral Significance. Musical Offerings, 1(1), 11–19. https://doi.org/10.15385/jmo.2010.1.1.2

CHAPTER FOUR

A Fictionalized Account of the Invention of the Piano, Interrupted by a Modern Account of Playing It

1674

Nineteen years old, forearms covered with sawdust up to the elbows, Bartolomeo stepped back from the harpsichord he had constructed with his father and looked it up and down. The woodwork was relatively even, though his father had admittedly taken the lead on that. But the ebony and ivory keytops were the clear focal points of the instrument, the keys screaming for attention before they even made a sound.

Bartolomeo stretched out his arm, feeling every joint and muscle awaken as he slowly reached for the harpsichord. As long as his father was in the room, he didn't dare play it. But touching was allowed; this he could pass off as inspecting the quality of the instrument. And inspect he did. The pads of his fingers travelled over every bump and groove on the instrument, his mind alive with thoughts of pressing his fingers into the keys and allowing the sound to swallow the workshop whole.

But testing the instruments was his father's job. Bartolomeo, his father had decided, could not be trusted with this task; for him, testing the harpsichord wandered dangerously into the realm of playing it. And Signor Cristofori would not have a musician for a son—this much was clear.

"Bartolomeo," his father said, gesturing towards the harpsichord, "The first of our harpsichords that is surely more your handiwork than mine. I am extremely impressed. I shall fetch the duke to retrieve his instrument." And, just like that, Bartolomeo Cristofori was left in his father's dusty workshop, with only the harpsichord for company.

He scanned the room for something resembling a bench, quickly settling on a large wooden crate in the corner of the workshop. Once it was in place, he sat down and again began running his hands over the body of the instrument. But this time, after a shaky breath in and a whisper of reassurance to himself, Bartolomeo allowed his fingers to drop their weight onto the keys. The resulting sound was dissonant, even ugly, but Bartolomeo was not deterred. He chose other keys, and other combinations of keys, and other rhythmic patterns with which to press the keys. When the sound was sweet, Bartolomeo celebrated by attempting a different sound. And when the sound was of dishes crashing to the floor or wild dogs barking at night, Bartolomeo rallied by trying a new combination of notes. He could have sat there by the harpsichord all day.

He was attempting a melody with only the black keys when he heard a knock at the door to his father's workshop. He stopped suddenly, echoes of a D-sharp still ringing in his ears as he rose. It wasn't his father and the duke; his father would not have knocked. But this was hardly a comfort—it could have been a particularly nosy passerby, a neighbour with a noise complaint, or even his mother, coming up to the workshop with bread and well-wishes. Bartolomeo's body moved towards the door, independent from his still-paralyzed mind.

He opened the door just a miniscule, overwhelming crack. Immediately, he saw Elisa's loose, golden locks and exhaled. A neighborhood girl who had taken an interest in Bartolomeo's work, almost as much as she had taken an interest in his wavy hair and almond-shaped eyes, Elisa was not likely to tell Bartolomeo's father what she had heard (if she had even heard anything at all).

"Elisa," he greeted her, nodding and gesturing for her to enter.

"Bartolomeo," she responded, taking in every sight in the workshop before her eyes finally rested on him. "Did you and your father make this?" She asked, gesturing to the harpsichord.

Bartolomeo nodded. "More me than him this time, if you can believe it," Bartolomeo explained, with a level of eagerness that he might have found embarrassing under any other circumstances.

"May I play it?" Elisa asked.

Bartolomeo nodded. Elisa, unlike Bartolomeo, had been formally trained in the harpsichord. And, more than that, her ears understood its workings more than anyone else Bartolomeo had ever met. When she played, the rest of the world fell silent to listen. The hum of the populace in Padua was suddenly no louder than a whisper.

Bartolomeo himself didn't dare breathe until Elisa rose from the wooden crate and he could be absolutely certain that she didn't have more notes in store for him. "You must teach me how to play like that," Bartolomeo said after a long silence, his voice coming out more breathless than he had intended.

"Well, you must teach me how to build like that," Elisa replied. "If I could create a harpsichord like this for my own home, I am not convinced I would ever leave."

"You must buy one from my father, Elisa. I am sure he would give you a lower price."

Elisa sighed. "You know my family would never ask that of him. Your father is too honest and good a man to be offering anyone a lower price."

She sighed and collapsed back onto the crate, the instrument in front of her feeling so close and yet increasingly far away. Defeatedly, she tapped out a G. Then a second G, with more force behind it, fuelled by her passion for the instrument and her rage at never being able to call it her own. Then a third time, so slowly and lightly and sadly that her finger hardly made contact with the key.

And still, each time, G... G... G. The greatest flaw in his handiwork, Bartolomeo realized, was that Elisa's talent outpaced the instrument's capabilities, ten to one at least. Where she could play the same note with a hundred thousand different emotions steering the joints in her fingers, the harpsichord could only utter each note in the same way.

"Elisa," Bartolomeo began, "is there such an instrument that will ring out louder when you play it with more force? Or quieter when you hardly brush against it? Like a harpsichord that will allow you to play piano e forte?"

"Not to my knowledge," Elisa said. "But, it is you who builds instruments, not me. Surely you know if such a thing is possible."

2004

Henry was only five years old when he began playing the piano. His teacher was an older woman, with an unplaceable accent and a penchant for large hats. Her name began with a V, or maybe it was a T, and she had a pleasant little studio in the east end of the city.

During their first lesson together, his teacher asked him to demonstrate anything that he already knew about the piano. Sure, Henry said, and he demonstrated getting up and leaving the room.

During their second lesson together, his teacher showed him how to put his fingers on the keys. Elbows in front of his body, flat wrists, fingers slightly curved like ten tiny rainbows. This is the most important part, she told him. Naturally, he refused to play a single note for the entirety of the lesson; after all, he was mastering the most important part.

During their third lesson together, his teacher began teaching him how to identify notes on the piano. This is a C, she told him, just like the letter of the alphabet. Henry responded with a well-rehearsed quizzical frown. I don't know the alphabet, he told her. He was, of course, bluffing, but she had no way of knowing that.

Henry didn't show up for their fourth lesson together. At first, the teacher suspected traffic or transit delays, but, after almost twenty minutes, there was still no word from his parents. So, she removed the stack of books from the piano bench, which were set up for Henry to sit on, and began to play. Inventions and minuets and sonatas, andantes and allegros, 90s hits and movie soundtracks. The music twisted and turned, whispered and shrieked, wandered far away and eventually found its way back to the start. Then, a loud creak, and the opening of the studio door.

The teacher paused the intricate Liszt piece she was playing, only moments before it reached its resolution, and turned around. There was Henry, standing behind his parents, shy eyes full of wonderment, rather than their usual mischief. His parents gave simultaneous apologetic shrugs. He didn't want to come in today. Made all the excuses in the book. Was a nightmare to drag him here. But he's here now—are we too late for a lesson?

The teacher paused for a moment, letting the suspense hang in the air with the penultimate Liszt notes, before shaking her head and gesturing for Henry to come in. His parents let out a simultaneous exhale, as though they had truly expected his teacher to say no. But they hadn't, of course. Who could say no to Henry? They asked each other, as they made their way back to their car.

Meanwhile, the teacher was restacking the music books on her piano bench, making sure that Henry would have enough height to properly align himself with the piano.

"Can I play the song that you were playing?" Henry asked, watching his teacher search for music books of just the right thickness.

"Someday," his teacher said, "if you practice."

"Why not today?" Henry asked.

"I have something different lined up for today: a five note C-scale. But I will tell you a secret, Henry. If you can play the five note C-scale with all of the emotions in your heart, it will sound just as beautiful as the song I was playing when you arrived today."

"I don't believe you," Henry said, stealing a glance at the door and contemplating whether he could catch his parents' car if he ran fast enough.

"That is what makes the piano so special—you can play the same note a hundred thousand times with a hundred thousand different emotions steering the joints in your fingers, and the piano will utter each one in a different way."

1709

Ferdinando de' Medici, Grand Prince of Tuscany, stood at the doorway to Bartolomeo's workshop and watched the inventor cry.

"What is wrong?" He asked Bartolomeo, extending a somewhat awkward hand towards him and patting him on the shoulder.

Bartolomeo shook his head. "It's not what is wrong but what is right. For twenty-six years, the vision of this instrument has followed me, and everything that I have constructed has brought me pain for what it is not. Only now does my wildest imagination stand in front of me, and I wish my dear Elisa were in Florence to see for herself."

The Prince stared blankly at Bartolomeo, then shifted his gaze to take in the object of Bartolomeo's overwhelming affections—it looked to be an archicembalo of mediocre quality, certainly not the inventor's best work. The Prince looked back at Bartolomeo, who was now sobbing loudly.

"Forgive me, Cristofori, but this is... an archicembalo," the Prince said.

Bartolomeo shook his head violently, the dark waves of his hair falling in front of his eyes and absorbing his still-streaming tears.

"It is not an archicembalo," he responded, definitively, making eye contact with the Prince for a long moment.

Then Bartolomeo took a breath. "Well, it is an archicembalo," he corrected, "but it is an archicembalo unlike any other. When you touch the notes, it listens to your hand, and it makes the sound that your hand wants to make."

The Prince tilted his head to the side, wondering if the carer of his instruments was going insane. "I'm afraid I do not follow."

"You have as much power over this archicembalo as your

own voice. You can make any combination of sounds that you desire. You can play it piano e forte," Bartolomeo said.

The Prince's disbelief carried him straight to the instrument, and his hands were on the keys before his brain had finished processing the sentence. With a gentle, hesitant touch, he pressed his thumb down onto one of the keys.

The resulting sound was an unmistakable honey-like piano.

[NOTE: Bartolomeo Cristofori was a real person, who lived between the years of 1655 and 1731. He did invent the piano around the year 1709, while caring for the musical instruments of Grand Prince Ferdinando III de Medici. However, little more than this is known about Cristofori's life, and the above story is entirely a work of fiction.]

Works Cited

Britannica, The Editors of Encyclopaedia. "Bartolomeo Cristofori". Encyclopedia Britannica, 30 Apr. 2022, https://www.britannica.com/biography/Bartolomeo-Cristofori.

Powers, Wendy. "The Piano: The Pianofortes of Bartolomeo Cristofori (1655–1731)." In Heilbrunn Timeline of Art History. New York: The Metropolitan Museum of Art, 2000–. http://www.metmuseum.org/toah/hd/cris/hd_cris.htm (October 2003)